An Insubstantial Universe

poetry in celebration of George Eliot
on the bicentenary of her birth

edited by Edwin Stockdale and Amina Alyal

with an Introduction by Jane de Gay

Sponsored by the Leeds Centre for Victorian Studies

© Copyright the authors 2020
Published by Yaffle Press, 2020

https://www.yafflepress.co.uk/

All rights reserved. No part of this book may be copied, reproduced, stored in a retrieval system or transmitted, in any form or by any electronic or mechanical means without the prior permission of the copyright holder.

ISBN: 978-1-913122-13-3

Cover design: Lorna Faye Dunsire

Cover image: Sofi at SlamdunkArt

Typesetting: Mike Farren

I speak not as of fact. Our nimble souls
Can spin an insubstantial universe
Suiting our mood, and call it possible,
Sooner than see one grain with eye exact
And give strict record of it. Yet by chance
Our fancies may be truth and make us seers.
'Tis a rare teeming world, so harvest-full,
Even guessing ignorance may pluck some fruit.

Juan the poet in *The Spanish Gypsy (1868)*

Contents

Introduction

Mary Ann Evans, Mary Anne Evans, Marian Evans, Mrs Marian Lewes, Mrs George Lewes, Mary Anne Evans Lewes, Mrs John Cross – best known as George Eliot – was an enigmatic figure who created memorable and compelling characters. Maggie and Tom Tulliver, the estranged brother and sister who are reunited as they drown in a flood; tragic dairymaid Hetty Sorrel whose beauty leads her to an ill-advised affair and love-child with dashing Captain Donnithorne; outcast Silas Marner who finds his redemption in golden-haired orphan Eppie; earnest Dorothea Brooke whose intellectual curiosity leads to a marriage with dry-as-dust Mr Casaubon before finding happiness, but not wealth, with Will Ladislaw: all these have captured the imaginations of readers for decades.

This collection presents a set of poetic responses to George Eliot's life, works, and landscapes, written during the bicentenary of her birth. It harnesses two research strengths of Leeds Trinity University: Creative Writing and Victorian Studies. Leeds Trinity is rapidly establishing itself as a centre of excellence for Creative Writing, generating a thriving community of writers through an annual Writers' Festival, a monthly open mic evening Wordspace, a series of annual publications under the Wordspace imprint, and BA, MA and PhD programmes. This collection includes work by members of this community, and others. Some poems were individually solicited, and others were selected from responses to a public call for submissions. The Leeds Centre for Victorian Studies, which sponsors this volume, has a twenty-five-year reputation as an internationally-recognized centre of excellence in the discipline, running conferences, seminars and colloquia, publications, including the *Journal of Victorian Culture*, as well as MA and PhD programmes. Well known for its interdisciplinary focus, it is being relaunched in 2020 to draw in an even wider range of subject areas and to reconsider the concept of the Victorian for the twenty-first century. As the first collaboration between Creative Writing and Victorian Studies, this volume extends disciplinary boundaries; it plays with chronological boundaries by reimagining a key Victorian figure from a twenty-first-century perspective.

Mary Ann Evans was born on 22 November 1819 in Nuneaton, Warwickshire in Arbury Farm (now South Farm) on the estate of Arbury Hall, where her father Robert (a former carpenter) was estate manager. Although she moved in infancy to Griff House on the road between Nuneaton and Coventry, the Arbury estate remained a playground for her, along with her brother Isaac, to whom she was very close. Eliot grew up in a rural area that was close to England's mining heartlands, and she captured the midlands landscape and its industrial struggles in many of her works.

Mary Ann Evans challenged the expectations of the era, especially for her gender, from a young age. She was a bright child who excelled at school, with the encouragement of her father, and even when she had to take on traditionally female domestic duties after her mother's death when she was sixteen, she nonetheless studied Italian, German, Greek and Latin with tutors. She rebelled from her family in matters of religion. She was Calvinistic at school, adopting a simple Puritan dress style that offended her brother, and then she began to distance herself from Christianity after moving to Coventry in 1841 and meeting Charles and Cara Bray, who introduced her to intellectuals such as Herbert Spencer, Harriet Martineau and R.W. Emerson. Now known as Marian Evans, she translated David Friedrich Strauss's *The Life of Jesus Critically Examined* (1846) which saw Jesus as human, not divine. Her religious views upset her father, though as a compromise she continued to attend church while he was alive. Throughout her life, she explored religious questions about death and immortality in works such as her poem 'The Choir Invisible' and her novella 'The Lifted Veil'.

After her father's death in 1849, Marian Evans visited Europe with the Brays, staying with François D'Albert Durade, who painted one of her most famous portraits, and after returning to Britain she moved to London in 1851, becoming part of a widening circle of sceptical thinkers. She met Charles Dickens, Charles Darwin, Wilkie Collins and Karl Marx, and produced a great deal of radical journalism anonymously as assistant editor of *The Westminster Review*. Through this group she met George Henry Lewes, with whom she lived from 1854 until Lewes's death in 1878. They could not marry because he was unable to obtain a divorce from his wife, and this unconventional lifestyle led to Eliot being ostracized by society and disowned by her brother. In 1863, Eliot and Lewes moved to the Priory, near Regent's Park, 1863, which became a salon for visiting intellectuals, thence to The Heights, near Weybridge. They travelled widely, with lengthy stays in Germany and Italy, visiting Florence, which inspired her historical novel *Romola*, and Rome, the setting for Dorothea and Casaubon's unhappy honeymoon in *Middlemarch*.

Evans adopted the pseudonym George Eliot when she began writing fiction, starting with the short story 'The Sad Fortunes of the Rev. Amos Barton', published first in *Blackwood's Magazine* and then as part of the collection *Scenes from Clerical Life* (1858). She then published a series of novels set in the Midlands: *Adam Bede* (1859), in which the hero is a carpenter, like her father; *The Mill on the Floss* (1860), a strongly autobiographical work, where the relationship between Maggie and Tom may be seen to reflect her relationship with her brother; and *Silas Marner: The Weaver of Raveloe* (1861). Eliot then published *Romola* (1863), set in Renaissance Florence and inspired by her Italian travels and drawing on wide-ranging research in history, theology, and art history. Her next novel, *Felix Holt: The Radical*, set amidst the reform movement of the 1830s, was highly pertinent to current debates about extending the franchise in 1866 – although women did not get the vote during Eliot's lifetime. *Middlemarch: A Tale of Provincial Life* followed in 1872, while Eliot's last novel, *Daniel Deronda* (1876) presented a more detailed and more sympathetic view of Judaism than was common at the time.

George Eliot married John Cross in May 1880, seven months before her death on 22 December that year. They honeymooned in Venice, where Cross jumped into the canal while suffering a breakdown. Nonetheless the marriage was the start of Eliot's rehabilitation: it mended her relationship with her brother, who wrote to congratulate them, and Cross went on to establish Eliot as an eminent Victorian by writing her *Life* (1885). Eliot was buried next to Lewes at Highgate Cemetery, in the Dissenters' Area because of her religious views and her adulterous lifestyle, but a plaque was placed in Poets' Corner, Westminster Abbey on the centenary of her death.

Many of the events in Eliot's life, described above, are explored imaginatively and philosophically in poems in this collection. Other poems respond to the places where Eliot lived and travelled, exploring them as settings and inspirations for Eliot's work, but also places for reflection, inspiration and pilgrimage. The poems traverse between life and fiction and back again, just as Eliot does in her novels, and demonstrating Eliot's suggestion that 'by chance / Our fancies may be truth and make us seers,' as she writes in *The Spanish Gypsy* (the long narrative poem from which the title of this volume is taken). The poems reflect on the differences between the Victorian era and today, but they also bring George Eliot to bear on contemporary life, sometimes humorously and always with imagination, as many of the poets speculate on what George Eliot might think of our present age. Others explore the complex and shifting identity of a figure who moved between names and genders, and many poems celebrate Eliot's characters, who have become friends and companions and have shaped lives. All the poems in this collection bear witness to what Anna Kisby sums up so beautifully: 'Dead poets / live forever you know.'

Reverend Professor Jane de Gay
Co-Director of the Leeds Centre for Victorian Studies

Tight lacing

George Eliot is waist deep in whale bone.
George Eliot is held precisely in place

by a whale's ribs. George Eliot is drifting
from room to room with the sea at her sides,

her own ribs horizontal, the whale's ribs vertical
and George Eliot sings, and the whale sings:

oh let me drift from room to room,
trees creaking under my feet,

the bone in the china rattling with every step,
fossils living it up in the limestone walls.

I'd swear every pane of glass is part
of the seventh wave, stretching me out,

cutting me down to size, my waist now
a full moon, my waist now an hourglass.

Then there's the ink, and the paper under the ink.
I will sit upright in the whale's mouth

and make smalltalk. I will push the whale
back into the waves and I will be the toast of London,

whale swelling lighted tapers we see by,
whale inventing its own improbable colour.

My name is Marian Evans. There is a dark shape
underneath our boat. One careless flick

and we'll be floating in the wreck of the drawing room,
chaise longues, billiard tables, a writing desk.

Poor Jonah dripping wet in evening dress.
Poor Noah, seasick and mucking out the bison.

My ribs match the horizon. My writing comes
in wave after wave. I follow True North.

I sing and the whales sing with me.
I overturn boatload after boatload

of shooting parties, whist drives.
Look at the bones like splints around

our own bones. Look at us standing around
like scrimshawed friezes. I am George Eliot

and the whales taught me everything I know.
I am Marian Evans and I am coming up for air.

Ian Harker

Maggie Tulliver saved

I swam away from Eliot's pen.
She was writing my death because
her time had run out for my story.

She wrote of the world she knew
but my head bobbed up from the river
in a different time.

My water-logged Victorian clothes
I sent back with the stream.
Who wants to wear such skirts?

They restrict. I will not be caged
nor coffined. I stride away
from the water's edge, into a future.

Call me Malala, call me Greta.
I will not be silenced. I have things to say
that will shake your world.

Angela Topping

The world's wife

But there is such a strain of poetry to relieve the tragedy that the more
she cries and the readers cry, the better I say.
G.H.Lewes. Letter to John Blackwood *(March 1860)*

This hair will not curl, too much of her father;
not the brains of her brother. This girl
should be seen, not heard, but she twitters,

too much fuss over butter. Little wench,
dark child, she hacks at her hair, spites her mother.
Books aren't for her; learning is men's work,

she'd do well to remember. Her place
is at home where the wheel sucks the Floss in,
spits it out again, turns days into years.

She grows uglier, hungrier. She should sit still,
content, but she runs, arms and legs,
through fields high with summer. Drifts off

with one who is meant for another; her cousin.
Comes back with her head up, no shame.
The Mill locks its doors, just herself to blame.

And now she is dead, God forgive her.
She slips without sound, her arms round her brother.
The end round these parts comes in water.

Gill Lambert

Childhood in St Oggs

Morton, Lincolnshire

Where the Trent veers, though I never asked why,
  by a small wharf, a row of Dutch-style houses,
dredge mounds – or high Viking burial mounds –
  in the play-world of conquering children,

slumped, rough mill-stones hidden in the hedges,
  God's dropped pennies, rolled from *The Mill on the Floss*,
a few barges, like squat messengers from the past,
  moving as slowly as the whole county,

secret tunnels of the brandy smugglers,
  the Lord of Stained Glass, the scabbed and scuffed knees,
our quacks and barks down dog-and-duck lanes,
  no full sloops come, no full sloops go.

Seth Crook

Dunstan's end

So he stepped forward into the darkness. – Silas Marner *(1861)*

Gaps in the blackthorn and bryony scrub of the hedge
lead downwards to well-trodden, half-hidden paths
deeper and deeper. In the long drought of summer
I duck in, out of the sun. You can wend down and down
along bumpy trails over leaf-buried spoil heaps –
it looks as if kids use it as a speedway for trail bikes
although I've never met any – until you're at the bottom
in deep mud at the pond's edge, and the dog plunges in,
stands half-submerged, and heaves out dripping black.

In winter the dark pool turns uncanny.
It rises with the rain, and seems to want you
to slip on the narrow path above and fall
helpless, past moss-hung limestone strata
to be gathered into the stonepit's oubliette.

Sarah Watkinson

The haunting of Silas Marner

Silas was paid in gold, and drew forth his gold,
long ago. Silver bore no large proportion in amount
to the gold, because the long pieces of work were
always partly paid for in gold. It had a gold handle,
deep letters on that gold handle. His heart warmed
over his gold, growing greed and worship of gold.
His gold. Silas's guineas were a golden wine.

His gold was gone. Had he put his gold
somewhere else? Didn't the gold lie? His gold
was not there. Restore the gold, get back his gold,
his gold. Before he lost his gold, it might have seemed
that so withered and shrunken a life as his
fidgeted incessantly with her lace, ribbons, and
gold chain – the little golden head, gold on the floor.

Gold! His own gold, the heap of gold, rubbing
the golden curls and kissing them. The child
was come instead of the gold: the gold had turned
into the child, unlike the gold which needed nothing.
The gold had kept his thoughts, the gold had asked
that he should sit, utterly crushed at the very first
by the loss of his long-stored gold.

His gold had departed. Who had taken her
golden curls? There's my gold-handled hunting-whip,
with my name on. Lay the recovered gold, the old,
long-loved gold. You might be changed into the gold
again. I seemed to see the gold; and I thought
old-fashioned gardens showed their golden and purple
wealth, and her hair looked like the dash of gold on a lily.

Oz Hardwick

Poem comprised of every phrase containing the word gold in *Silas Marner* (1861),
in order. Punctuation and lineation added.

The man from Raveloe

he never minded   being lonely
for that was
     the way all things became

he was just   a bit early

     lights
            colours
                  dust below

dissatisfaction is   an illness
and he   had tried so hard to be well

     sounds
        fog
         clouds above

when you weave   it is not the hand   but the thread
that makes the art
so   even he could make
something beautiful   and not so lonely

     empty ground
           beneath
            the house

he only ever   asked for little
yet when young eyes   see
they make   everything seem
     so large

when you weave   it is the thread   not the hand
     that shapes you
he had been   malleable as gold
     left in the sun

Adriana Grigore

Return to Raveloe

Behind the shutters it was a dingy, cramped book; the cottage and its faded weaver an interlude on the path to O Level. Myopic as Silas himself, I fumbled through, in order to escape Raveloe forever. But forty years later, the village welcomes me on the first page with *the rapid use of that difficult instrument the tongue*. I laugh aloud, shudder. Yes, it's a woman's finest: buttering, slicing, lashing.

The women charm me. I marvel at Mrs Osgood scooting past, discreet and resolute, as if she has *little wheels to her feet*. I bask in Mrs Crackenthorp's blinks, her guinea pig squeaks and twitches; there always is a woman whose fidgetings are contagious.

And Dolly *Oh dear, dear* Winthrop. Auntiest of aunts, comfort-ladler, death-and-disaster warden – Dolly appears on the doorstep, and within the hour sets our knotted life whirring again like a loom. Unwrapping her bundle, I'm saddened that she cannot decipher the letters (copied from the pulpit-cloth) she's pricked onto her spiced lard-cakes. I could tell Dolly I spent years teaching vibrant women to read. Instead I listen to her homespun sense: *And all as we've got to do is to trusten.*

Molly Farren, tramping white dark lanes, is beyond the world of Dolly's ministry. I agonise – isn't there a shred of Molly in all of us? The need to fall into a soft warm bed of opium, and sleep, sleep. I track her daughter specking across the snow – *a little starved robin*, laudanum's orphan. At Silas's hearth, Eppie is granted a second birth.

At last I come to Nancy Cass's quiet house, where *there are no voices calling her away from that soliloquy*. She bears her loss – I see this now – as if it were near to grace. But if a woman stops visiting a drawer, or clears it, the drawer remains. I wish she would describe the missing garment, a miniature hand-stitched burial dress. We share a fear of *cherishing a longing for what was not given*. She might have read me then, forty years ago. I should have lingered with Nancy.

Anne Ryland

Notes from *Notes on* The Mill on the Floss

I

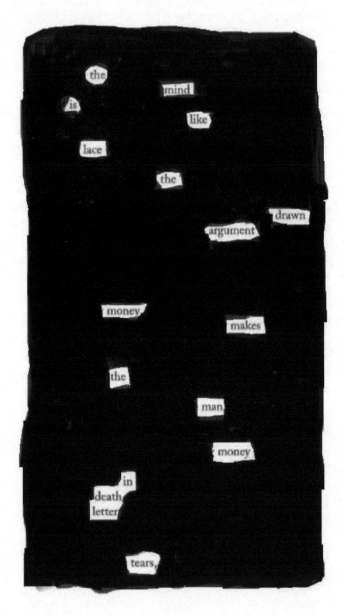

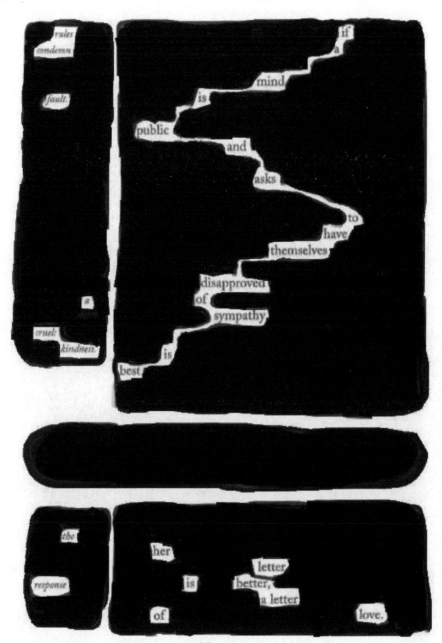

II

rules
condemn   if
                            a
fault.   mind
              is
        public
              and
                asks
                      to
                    have
              themselves
        disapproved
        of
              sympathy
  a
cruel:
  kindness.   is
best

the
        her   letter
response   is   better,
                    a letter
        of   love.

III

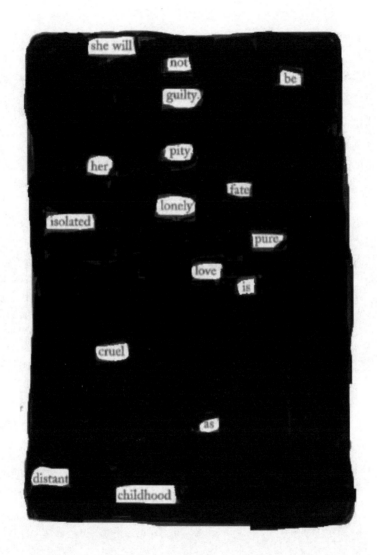

she will
not
be
guilty.
pity.
her
fate
lonely
isolated
pure
love
is
cruel
as
distant
childhood

Joe Williams

Source text: Griffin, N. (1988), *York Notes: The Mill on the Floss*. London: York Press.

The mother I would have liked

Mrs Craig takes me to the library, points me towards
Captain Ahab, D'Artagnan, Allan Quatermain.

She lends me her clothbound edition of *Mill on the Floss*.
I bond with Maggie Tulliver –

Maggie knows what it's like to have a mother
who can only imagine her daughter as a wife.

Mother whines in bursts like the hoover,
You'll never find a man with your straight-as-a-broomstick hair.

She perms my hair too tight,
I look ridiculous! I spit. She doesn't care what I say.

Like Maggie, I hack at my hair. Mother spits,
You look ridiculous! I don't care what she says.

I rush to Mrs. Craig's.
She listens, strokes what remains of my hair.

Veronica Aaronson

Maggie Tulliver comme moi

She was, like me, *trop spontanée*
pour observer les conventions.
Too spontaneous. She wanted

to wear a red kerchief and tell
the Roma – hiding her anguish –
about Columbus and Geography.

Her sister Fedalma, troubadour-led,
jewelled, stamped with her dancing feet
on the aching pate that she sprang from

fully-formed, a changeling, drowning
in *the chilling snow* that dowsed
the *fire within* – muffled, muted,

in the mores of post-Moorish Spain.
Called towards Carthage – *We rebelled –*
the larger life subdued us – she resigned

a life. Yet jewels and dancing beckoned.
Maggie knew that call and its toll. Perhaps
Marian's psyche too feared hypoxia

for fashioning her own *vie Bohème*,
fleeing Coventry to be sent right back,
but the real price of defiance internal.

Amina Alyal

Quotations in French from Simone de Beauvoir, *Le deuxième sexe* (1949).
Reference is made to *The Spanish Gypsy* (1868) in lines 7-16.

Red cloth and epaulets

Her favourite poem was Lalla Rookh
so Rosamond Vincy wove her dreams
and went forth to greet the King of Bukhara
only to bump into a poet
whose songs were so sweet
she swooned away and found alas
king and poet are not always the same.

The business of her life was furniture,
her aim to fill her married home
with silver and plate and baubles,
polished tables, gilded mirrors
which did not bring out her pretty smile,
only reflected how she saw herself
when accomplishments were not enough.

Carole Bromley

Wanting the Will

He was not there like a summer storm,
but like a Picasso portrait among gentle landscapes,
Will Ladislaw, rich with feeling, warm.

Some of us have the will to be like Will, we pray
one day heads will turn and people say,
He's not like us, he's interesting, an eclipse,
or perhaps a foreboding cloud on a summer lawn.
Some of us long to kiss those lips,
and some regret that they were born
in that changeless English society
where they worship God and sobriety.

But my first taste of the writer – him and her
was in those three weeks of my student life,
when my mind went around the mean streets
wanting the will to be Will and cause a stir.

Stephen Wade

Radical

After Felix Holt, the Radical *(1866)*

Like most words, it can mean just what you want –
mean Holt or Transome: honest artisan
or landed gentleman and buccaneer
capitalist, who wants you to believe
that he'll defend your interests, although
his own lie in preserving family wealth.

It's politics and everybody's mad
as hell, people are sicced on one another,
some die, while others wake up wondering
how they got sore heads and a broken knuckle.
It's just the game of changing leaders' names
and making sure you keep real change at bay.

Of course, true and pretend radical lose
for now, although we know reform will come –
had come, three decades-odd before she wrote –
and more was coming, like a rising tide
old money might hold back a few more years
but in the end is irresistible.

Mike Farren

Transfusion
After The Lifted Veil *(1859)*

If the ink in my pen is
the blood jet

(as our sister Sylvia said)

then with this transfusion
we bring Mary Ann back to life.

Dead poets
live forever you know.

Anna Kisby

Arbury Hall, Dusk, Sometime in the 1820s

Under fan vaulting wanders a girl: stout boots, calico skirts, a doll hammered to her heart. In the dark dining room, red velvet chairs loom like punctuating pools of blood. And the setting sun raises a lantern's flicker in the elegant mirror and the glassy expanse of the table. In shady niches under arches lurk old images of forgotten saints, found long ago in Italy. Sometimes there's a mountain landscape, wild with stormy oils, and anguished trees, bit through with bitumen. The hall's a sea of shining chequered tiles, all black and white, beneath a winding stair which climbs to endless chambers, full of night. You'll need a candle – and some courage – to go there. The gallery windows let in the dusk. Dark eyes watch in the pale faces of the long-dead Newdegates, locked forever in their portrait frames. In unused rooms where no fire ever makes a merry heat upon the hearth, stands shrouded furniture in sheets, a silent herd of ghosts. The library is bare-boarded, and dead Sir Roger's desk is like a tomb. The pungent odour of decaying books, with esoteric wisdom, hangs like leathery incense in the air. Fleeing back into the basement, where the servants are, in a passageway she waits a while; a tallow candle sheds a cheap and cheerful light on whitewashed walls. She finds a tiny painting, exiled from the cold white Gothic splendours up above. A scene of peasants drinking in the sun: they dance and dally with a smiling wench. The flickering warmth of a fire shines out from the housekeeper's room, washing the wall and rustics with a rosy glow. The sound of common voices, sharp with the small news of the parish and old stories of the house draw in the girl to bread and milk, and tales.

Rosemary Mitchell

Dorothea on Marriage

*The long vistas and wide fresh air which she had dreamed of finding in
her husband's mind were replaced by ante-rooms and winding
passageways which seemed to lead nowhither.* – Middlemarch *(1871-72)*

Leather creaks. Casaubon shifts his weight,
leans forward over his desk. I smell pipe smoke,
a faint tinge of brandy. Damp is rising,
foxing piles of papers in the corners of his library.

I sense his mind inching forwards. Then digressing.
Sometimes I picture him as a matron looking
for lost *keys to all mythologies* in the back of a drawer.
When we were in Rome, he scolded, 'Dorothea,

you are all appetite. Too impetuous. Too quick.'
I felt like a hungry child on my wedding night:
offered a plate of dry crackers when I dreamt
of summer pudding plump with sugared fruit.

Our marriage, I fear, is a crumbling manor –
dust-sheeted for the winter, windows
shuttered from natural light. The meat hooks
in the larder are empty of game or sides of beef.

Soon he will light a taper, make his measured
way up to his bedchamber. His heart's weak;
each knee-joint encrusted with arthritis.
I have retreated to the east wing of the house.

My bedroom ticks and sighs as the fire dies down.
I long for another body's warmth! Dream of the soft,
feathered breasts of wood pigeon and partridge.
I live in an underworld of my own making.

Outside, the sombre yews, the avenue of limes,
begin to crystallise and freeze.

Anne Caldwell

The Canals of Venice

16 June 1880

Johnny: his bowtie lips with the turned-down crease at the corners, his heavy-lidded sensual eyes, tracings of facial hair on his chin and sideburns. Her skin craves his touch. On the grand balcony studying the aquamarine depths from the many-curved edges of the water, she reaches for his hand. He flinches, says, 'Not here.' He stalks inside. The sun is a lime, fermented.

*

Returning to the honeymoon suite she catches Johnny, twenty years younger than her, making love with another man. She makes her exit, stumbles, steadies herself on the wooden door. In her head, she says: *there will always be pale sad faces among the flowers, and eyes that look in vain.*

*

Johnny lies between the sheets, waiting for her. She laughs, says, 'Dearest, I married you for companionship.'

*

In the looking-glass she traces the lines around her mouth, thinks they are distinguished. She reviews her softened reflection. She kisses him full on the lips; he backs away.

*

He jumps into the canal, to drown himself in the tourmaline expanse of unstable water.

Edwin Stockdale

———————————

Some words and phrases are taken from *Romola* (1862-63), such as *many-edged*, *there would always be pale sad faces among the flowers, and eyes that look in vain*, *softened reflection* and *unstable*.

21

Choices

I am looking at a portrait of George Eliot. I am also seeing your face, Maggie: the blue-eyed, inquisitive face of a soulful horse. The face a hunchback loved along with the heart it expressed: the face that narrated itself into every drop of mill-water whilst its eyes squinted – long – at parchment next to candlelight.

> *Or I could be perching awkwardly on crumbling masonry, knees dirty from the clamber. Straining to hear as distant cousins endlessly eviscerate one another's mothers in neat parlours.*

We are in the water with the mad mill-owner's daughter. The currents swirl around as the narrator reaches down her bony fingers to stir all our prejudices, guilt and blame. Judge her, judge her – you must! Then judge me. The quill stills and the rolling locks droop over the long, exquisite features.

> *Or we could be holding the outstretched paper wings of an impossible angel as her blameless demise flutters the pages into a pool of tears, mingled with the author's finer feelings, naturally.*

The flood of human emotion is unstoppable. Under the surface, light diffracts in sharp angles amidst the eddies. Maggie breaks free for an instant, her George-Eliot-horse-face illuminated in a mask of anguish: more alive than any heroine before, so more truly dead.

> *Or we could be staring through the window at weird, bleak, solipsistic young women torturing themselves into patterns of death and remembrance while dark fantasies blossom outwards.*

We'll drown with you, Maggie Tulliver.

Paul Coleman

Not divided

I always knew she would drown in the Floss.
When she was little I expected it —

late back for tea — drowned
fallen out with Tom — drowned
run off with gypsies —

I wished her bonnier
and gentler, not so quick,
more like myself, my sisters,
her cousin Lucy.

In the end she was quite the beauty,
drew men's eyes.

In the end it wasn't only Maggie.

Dead
              like their father.

I wouldn't wish her bonny now,
                 just quick,
her and my handsome boy.

Jean Taylor

2019

I bunked off uni when we did *Middlemarch*.
There was a pool tournament at the Fenton
and I had to get some game time in.
I spent each night in the pub the week before,
went through students like students go through pasta
and the week after, potted my way to the final.
I was up against Nigel, the landlord.
First prize: twenty pints! I got five
as a runner up. Nigel thrashed me 7–1.
It was the best of 9. I conceded
so I could sink my second prize by closing time.

I got around to *Middlemarch* in her bicentennial year,
watched tensions rise between Dorothea
and Casaubon while they honeymooned in Rome.
I saw a reverend control his wife beyond his death
to stop her marrying the man she loved
by depriving her of her inheritance.
But unlike me and my obsession with green-baize glory,
at least there was a happy end to Dorothea's story.

Mark Connors

Highgate Cemetery

Taking the tarmacked path
I noticed chestnut trees,
gold in sunlight, after
many days of rain.

I thought about who planted them:
a heart-broken lover?
a schoolboy prank on a master?
a squirrel's careless hoard?

These majestic trees
now dwarf the dead
whose standing in life
was measured by size of memorial.

Witch-hazel, a symbol of sorrow,
cypress denotes lamentation,
chestnuts – a carpet of seed cases
reveals harvest is complete.

Are souls reaped for harvest
and planted anew?
The neatly tied durex suggests
life triumphs amongst gravestones.

Here Mary lies next to her soulmate,
together in life, together in death,
wagging tongues silenced,
leaving *The Choir Invisible* as their solace.

Trees celebrate autumn, praise sunlight,
awaiting rebirth like characters
who live again when we open
George Eliot's books and read.

Clint Wastling

Highgate Cemetery 1878

Your pathos is better than your fun – George Henry Lewes

unspeakably
    everlasting winter has set in
the moon's dull
November eyes offer no warmth
        I do not know why I speak to you out loud
wishing you to deny
this pollution of nature
                     & rise against gravity
tighten your fingers into mine
        you appear in the veins of a falling leaf
catching my breath I allow darkened clouds
            of you to blow through

now I have to face the faces exuding femininity
who accept invitations to dinner parties
          display their sateen vanity
            & refuse to question why
    they run their finger down the index of me
searching in vain for all the folly
         of lady-like behaviour

I desire eyes to look love on me
I am a bruised creature
      a perpetual mourner

life has lost its eagerness
I miss our illicit kisses
        our scandalous morality

depend upon it

Kathleen Strafford

Nom de Plume

In the days when young husbands leapt
    from balconies in flapping great coats
but failed to turn into ravens or doves
    and God-fearsome moralists would spin
like bobbins upon the illegitimate gravestones
    of their fathers' good names, when
the lanes in far off districts were dotted
    with disinherited wanderers trailing
suspicion like gun smoke from the choking
    battlefields of decaying quarrelsome monarchs,
Mary surmised that both subjugation and suffrage
    were mysterious but entirely necessary burdens
in a bag of good reason that held nothing,
    to some, but coils of flaxen thread, but to her
instruments to fathom conditioning and conscience,
    and if God was anywhere he, or she, or nix
slept away a hidden life in a downy nest
    high up in a tree, deep in the bosom
of the Swiss Alps, unperturbed by the Autumn
    thunder that rolled among the peaks,
as if it were only the bluster of an aging father,
    head of the household, losing his temper,
yet again, over the lack of piety and proper
    decorum in his offspring; but how
the feather-name of George, as it shall be,
    was such a good mouth-filling word
somehow solid, like stone, when uttered.

Bob Beagrie

In Father's drawing room

Monotony of surface & of form
Without a break to hang a guess upon. – from In a London Drawingroom

I've seen it stitched in many rooms:
'Home is where the…' but oh, that's trite,
perhaps it is not the platitude of *home*
that offends me so, home is, home is,
home is wherever Father hangs his hat
or our maid lays the fire –
I'd venture any of those as given fact.
Home is where I hang my guess
on all I am yet to be, still a mould-held,
unset flummery of a thing. That is not
to say I am miserable with my lot or that
I find no pleasure in a job nicely done,
but a home falls short when its walls
mind-encroach, like trellis-seekers taking
more than their fair share of space and light.
There are no drops I could take to cure
the skull-stifled same, same old. I can amble
out of doors, through the yard-gate of books
but wouldn't it be something to take liberty
for granted. If only thought were a ball I could throw
just to see how far it goes, without the monotony
of chores, without concern for duty or appearances,
to compromise my aim.
If I were free to scrutinise Him as earnestly
as tonight's menu, if my musings were as important
as my *toilette*. If my home were my own,
not clod-sunk but set on wheels, I could move it
as I liked, catch a fresh view daily, no usual place
on the pew, just Home trundling
forwards, forwards – towards the new.

Jo Brandon

I am lonely

And I am lonely... – I am Lonely

My body breaks into a house for prayer.
A nightingale sings the future like a soothsayer.
The flow of the night breaks at dawn.

My body breaks into a house for redemption.
My bone and flesh refuse an amalgamation.
Lost is the joy expected at dawn.

My body breaks into a house of broken things.
My mind drowns in the waters of fallen kings.
The sea rises to begin waving at dawn.

My body breaks into a house for slaughter.
It no longer recognizes the taste of water.
The sun dies again to rise at dawn.

Temidayo Jacob

Elsewhere

When light prods
at the curtain   you look up
having been away
to a place where the news
did not exist
and the journey was calm
for these waters
                    Yet you
sense you've not travelled
enough   wish you'd tipped
over the horizon   known something
of the bend in the world

Katrina Naomi

Fire and rain

He seemed to weave, like the spider, from pure impulse, without reflection. – Silas Marner *(1861)*

My country lanes and fields,
the round pond and pages,
words of worlds outside,
bring fire and rain to my heart,
the joy of each native flower,
the bittersweet, enchanter's nightshade,
the biting stonecrop.

I'm Mary Anne with an E,
E for emotional. I loved my schooling mother,
her soft skin and conversation.
I'm Mary Ann without an E
an E that longs for love, shape-shifter
in petticoats and aprons.

I don't cry. I nursed my parents,
held their dying hands. I don't cry.
I love the kitchen. I make currant jelly,
mince pies and damson cheese. I pat the butter.

I'm Marian, a portrait with kind eyes
and scruffy hair, a pen and mouth
like no other woman. I can be your lover,
your philosopher lost in the arms of my ghosts.

I'm George Eliot, some other being cocooned by love.
I'm cast away from all you followers
of tight-lipped views; I'm cast away.

I'm Polly, yours for always,
My fortune, our hearts together, my words
and chapters from the soil, the churning dairy
of worlds, the touch of a weaver's shuttle.
These stories are yours and mine.

I'm the other woman, full of love and grief,
something left of me under this gravestone.
I'm Mary Ann Cross: something strange
in your small world, my globe bigger
now I'm gone, now I'm just fire and rain.

Penny Sharman

The toil of George Eliot

Why so unsung? Was it the lack
of convention? Austen, a following,
offers satisfaction, the Brontës
an industry, but for Eliot silence,
as if her offer dissatisfaction.

Father aghast at her dropping
religion, brother in turn
for her *living in sin*,
Lewes unable to get divorced,
she made her pitch writing.

And what of the Queen:
did Victoria know, or care,
how her favourite author lived?
Dreamed, maybe, of John Brown
or her Indian trusty?

New century, Virginia Woolf
viewed things perceptively:
Geo. Eliot, shrinking from fame,
retreating into the arms of love,
her face expressing sullen power.

All just ferreting! *Middlemarch*
the real thing: Dorothea hopeful,
fazed by Casaubon's nit-picking,
Lydgate's own aspirations also
derailed by marriage.

A tale of individuals,
their aims, foibles, setbacks,
played out in a panorama:
nation-wide and over decades
from Georgian to Victorian.

Deronda a portmanteau book,
Marner sombre till near its end,
Maggie of *The Mill on the Floss*
losing out like Eliot. And so on:
it's left down to *Middlemarch*.

Simon Currie

To S.H., a letter (removed)

Each letter has been pruned of everything that seemed to me irrelevant to my purpose – of everything that I thought my wife would have wished to be omitted. – J.W. Cross, 'Preface' *to his edition of* George Eliot's Life, as related in her Letters and Journals (1885).

Beloved Achates, the companion in my exile
from those who should have loved me most,
let us rescue these letters
from the pyre that cleanses reputation.
Though I address you with the tongue of Virgil,
I confess that poetry rarely flowed from my pen.
Yet, in my prose, some lineaments of poesy reside,
like sinews and muscles which cling
to the bones beneath the skin of story.
You were she who sifted, with gentle hands,
the grain from the chaff of all I poured
from my well-garnered heart,
you the wise seraph whose breath of kindness
blew away what needed not to be kept.
You it was with whom I turned each leaf
of books which fed our souls, our minds,
with bushels of seedcorn to grind
for the harvest of our own writing.
You were the midwife to my early labour,
held in tender hands my stillborn faith,
you whose household nourished my infant novel
with wholesome sops, delighted in its faltering first steps.
My exile now is ended; Aeneas rests in the bosom
of a beloved spouse, yet will never forsake you,
the faithful friend of youthful days.
Write to me, as you did of old,
and I will cherish those crossed and crumpled pages
as if they were rare parchment fragments.

This I despatch from Venice,
and when I return, I will send again.

Hannah Stone

The poem includes quotations from George Eliot's own writings.

Auto-defenestration on the Grand Canal

While the heart beats, bruise it– The Lifted Veil

The much older bride,
serene at her desk

says: by sumptuary law
gondolas are painted black

Is it hot in here?
the jumpy groom asks

as he loosens his English collar.
The *gondolieri* sing

a siren song, he thinks,
walking to the beckoning balcony

overdressed and overfleshed.
He thought too little of the heat

between the open window
and watery temptation.

He lets the collar drop
into the foul canal below

and follows.

Terri Brandmueller

Marian Evans

To those who love her best
her landscape is in every sense flat.
Tiny increments grow and change,
rubbing against one another.

Industries are long gone,
food processing, cloth-making and mining.
Difference is all around us,
decentering the world.

Middlemarch immortalises us,
small-time farmers and ribbon manufacturers,
call centre managers and market gardeners,
in a hideous neighbourhood of ignorant bigots.

Take a second look at this place.
Rethink the value of your home.
Beauty and Ugliness collide there;
both bounce away from the centre.

Dreaming of an expanded existence,
rich characters here long to escape,
mortified by their regional accent,
stuck in the uncompromising provinces.

Glorious, highly profitable novels pour
from a country-dwelling gentle woman,
a paid-up member of the liberal metropolitan,
pseudonym George Eliot,

a kind of affirmatory magic
for inchoate longings
with the hope of another life,
intellectual, creative, purposeful,

clever girls of modest means and glamour,
cravings and clumsy local men,
living at the edge of middle,
viewed from a different perspective.

Someone more cosmopolitan enters,
no ageing pedant with ugly white moles;
a paid-up intellectual beckons.
Emotional flexibility thrives.

Supremely relational art endures.
Powerful, everyday, ordinary
Marian will never return.
Her success is in the City.

Gail Webb

This is a found poem from the *Guardian*, 16 November 2019.

Imago

"...and just against it I'll put in snowdrops and crocuses 'cause Aaron says they won't die out, but'll always get more and more."
"Ah child!" said Silas [...] "it wouldn't do to leave out the furze-bush" –
Silas Marner *(1861)*

Mary Ann debates with new friends,
windows misting
as conversation heats.
She filters and sifts,
flickering gold illuminating
a mesh of thought.

I watch my belly swell.
She will be mine, not mine.
Snug in her sac,
her limbs butterfly my stomach.

Marian paces up and down her room,
looks in the mirror at her plain, strong features.
She picks up her pen,
dashes off a letter to J.S. Mill, M.P.

At your first insistent suckle,
in the shape of your head I see Mum.
Damp whorls cling to your cranium pulse;
sharp pain tugs; tears and milk begin to leak.

My Mum, briefly paused from Consultant life,
watches Mary Poppins with me:
I sing, *Well done, Sister Suffragettes.*
ask, *What does it mean?*

Mary Ann, Marian, now George,
fights to preserve Wandsworth Common.
She looks from her window and worries
about the fading snowdrops,
the emerging lilac crocuses against the green.

My daughter, my Eppie,
borrowed my comb before leaving home.
I rescue our curls from its teeth,
gold threads woven with silver.
I hear her words, echoing mine, not mine,
I told my friends, women died so we can vote.

Jenny Robb

The quotation is from Part II, Chapter XVI, where Eppie and Silas discuss Eppie's
garden, to be created on the spot where her mother died.

Mary Ann Evans and I return to Nuneaton after some years away

We met at the train station.
She said she remembered it opening
which kind of set the baseline.
I asked if she used to go to the Tav
but she walked past it without a glance.

The George Eliot Hotel had St George's crosses hanging outside –
it's known as The George, I told her.
It was our first stop on a Saturday night –
a portrait of Larry Grayson used to hang in the lounge, might still.
She hadn't heard of Larry. I thought, shall I tell her

about the time I ran from my boyfriend's flat after an argument
and jumped in the new fountain in my nightshirt? Or after they built
      the ring road –
the night I peeled the kicking legs from the Rs on the road sign
while my friend peed behind a bush, and for years it was the Poanne
      Pingway?
Could I explain ringroads using the doctrine of consequences?

I took her through the George Eliot Gardens –
are you sure that's what they're called? she said –
then up the hill to the hospital – I wanted her to see for herself.
In the foyer a woman talked into her phone: *Gran's been moved to
      Dorothea Unit.*
Mary Ann looked at me in bewilderment

so I pointed to the list of wards
Daniel Deronda, Adam Bede, Felix Holt, Bob Jakin,
Mary Garth. I told her my daughter was born here.
But do they know who I am?
Let's go to the museum, I said.

On the way down the hill I said, *there's a road too,*
at least two schools, a board game.

I didn't read your books until after I'd left –
I thought you were a town worthy.
She didn't stop laughing until we were inside

and she was confronted with her own writing desk
her own shoes, her favourite cushion, her nightgown
pinned, labelled, arranged in glass cases.
My God! she said
I didn't think you believed in him, I replied.

She was a bit shaken so we went for a cup of tea in Asda.
I told her they'd named a range of clothes after her, but she didn't
         believe me.
Do they know I'm not a man? Do they know I wasn't married?
Nobody cares any more, I told her, *and I don't think many people*
         have read your books,
some don't even remember Larry Grayson.

                                                    Anna Chilvers

The new Middlemarchian

Are we to play Casaubon and Dorothea?
Is it my turn to attend to you, leaving you
free to dribble your seminal ideas,
your less than copious issue,
while I mop up your piddling product?
Shall I help your corpus slowly swell
while my own oeuvre starts to shrivel?
No. Now is the time to watch me act.
I'll shed my coat, split pod, cast seed,
and even as your words fall flaccid,
I'll prick mine out: sprout, spur, bud, chit
send tendrils out to probe the slits
you say your prose would rather not.
Now see how my stuff hits the spot.

Sharon Larkin

Life seems to go on without effort when I am filled with music

After The Mill on the Floss *(1860)*

Her funniest bone collided with her polished bannister rail.
It halted her in her bedtime climb, stopping still on her thirteenth
stair, to whine, inhale and wail.

But the bone song sound was hollow, like the beat she used to know
on her tight-as-hell-skinned bongo. A tune to make her calm again,
and to drown out all her pain.

Matt Nicholson

Hetty at the Pool

Tree branches fuse fragile surface tension,
a dark net to snare any anguished jumper,
night hiding innocence from its own awareness.
She is not yet twenty, but teeming lifetimes
shadow its depths. She chooses, disposes
of herself and her baby, a red cloak of despair
covering her clock-ticking urgency. She has suffered
long in the pain of her belly, and cold Nature
denies any recourse to justice. Larvae and caddis
dwell unharmed in its chill, but this girl slopes
away, undiscovered, to kill.

Sally Taylor

Hetty Sorrel waits

At seventeen, her face fills a Hall Farm window,
rose and alabaster, features no one forgets –
beauty she can't help but remind herself of
in polished pewter and speckled glass.
Look closer. Behind those gloss-black eyes
lies the pain of waiting, her world
a circle unclosed. Locket in hand, gift from their first tryst
recalled as a dream that stays all summer –
she sleeps, missing dawns lit by Memnon song,
guelder roses and purple daisies in early sun.
Hollow hours crave another taste
of his kiss, enclosed in a copse as dusk
shadows cloak shoulders of Binton Hills,
worlds away from dairy kitchen and kettle-cake.

Paul Waring

Becoming George

Prologue

This is the true tale of Mary Ann Evans:
devoted daughter, church-goer, housekeeper,
becoming George: writer, editor, stereotype bubble-
burster, with a good mouth-filling name.

Parados

Plain women must be devoted to education,
for who but plain scholars would want them?
She took her father's gift of disappointment
and lost her virginity to a satisfying book.

Episode

She believed in, well, tell them George...
"Literal truth, and realism over fantasy."
Down with females swooning over bulging prospects.
Bring on all-wrinkled realism. Snaggle-toothed
realism that leaves bite marks on your arms.
She was determined to be "a stranger on the earth."
An unbeliever, an odd child, a disjointed specimen,
like one of her lessons – Latin verbs and scraps of
poetry – as useful as if she had been born a boy.
She read, she critiqued, she radicalised, she wrote,
became Editor in all but name. And as Other Woman,
shared many honeymoons with a married man
who gave his name to her novelist's nom-de-plume.

Stasimon

They thought her a clergyman, a Cambridge man
a proud father and family man. A man who has seen
a great deal of society. A man with humane wisdom
to write the greatest novel in the English language.
Certainly not, most definitely not, no, never a woman.

Exodus

Laid to rest amongst societal outcasts, the woman with
a force of genius reserved only for men. The woman
who mapped her way beyond the gender dead ends,
and had her books on the bedside table of the Queen.
This beautifully bruised creature living a realist's dream.

Natalie Scott

Told as a mini Greek tragedy (because she loved those).

Maggie Tulliver encounters her inner Medusa

It was cruel, the morning I awoke
to feel them writhe and thrash,
a corona of dark serpents,
each with a life of its own,
sharing my pillow. My scalp crawled.

The more I tried to shrink
into myself, the more my coiffure
coiled and uncoiled itself, hissed
and spat, a nest of venomous vipers
which no comb could ever control.

Now these locks speak for me.
My own voice has been silenced
by the malevolence of this unruly hair.
Take away the mirrors, bring the shears!
I am already petrified by what I may become.

Barbara Farley

Silas

There had been a time when he was lonely,
thinking only of the next thread on the loom,
the weave of warp and weft, from dawn to dusk.
A living measured out by each transaction,
by coins he stashed beneath his flagstoned floor.
With Eppie at his side, his outlook changed:
the once familiar rendered strange, like cloth
viewed from the other side, life's patterns
now revealed in colour, shade and texture.
Transformed, his fingers fly across the loom,
as if enchanted. He has encountered love,
has learned to care once more. Tenderly
he wraps the cloth around his sleeping child,
sees precious gold only in her soft, warm curls.

Angi Holden

Six Portraits

1842, aged 22
Cara Bray

Cara made me curl my hair, so that part is false
but the rest, I concede, is honest: my big head,
high brow (enough intellect to keep the animal in check,
says Combe, pointedly)

and horse face – who else would own it?
But the cringing posture of a ten-year old – is that me?
She wants to be sure I am no threat to her Charles.
Too late. I have already caught his eye.

If only one could preserve those fleeting instants
when beauty, like sunlight, crosses the least propitious fields.
There is something between Charles and me
and it is not Cara's pencil.

1850, aged 30
Francois D'Albert Durade

Who is this demure, over-laced demoiselle –
plump, smiling, beatific? Durade has given me colour,
but I was a wraith when I turned up on his step.

Another zealous coiffeuse: symmetrical buns
over each ear, like some zoomorph. As he draws,
I try not to speculate on this intense little man.

Married life with him? The full face slims my nose
and chin, but is not me. Not Mary Ann Evans.
Marianne? 'Madame Marianne D'Albert Durade'.

His wife, Julie – I call her Maman – shares his bed
but not, surely, his passion for calculation.
I imagine myself in her shoes – then slip them off.

1858, aged 38
John Mayall

A second photograph? No, no, NO.
What use is the camera if it cannot lie?
This catches me cackling, scratching my jaw
like a demented harpy.

I don't need proof of my ugliness
from The London Stereoscopic & Photographic
        Company.
Mayall ordered dozens from the pimply youth.
No, I said. Burn the lot.

1860, aged 41
Samuel Laurence

Poor Laurence.
'He has made you look melancholy,' groans G.
Made me? I am my own woman.

G, with endearing solipsism,
wants the world to know he makes me happy.

Blackwood bought it and it hangs in the inner sanctum
of his office. I am moved.

1865, aged 46
Frederic William Burton

Good enough for the Royal Academy,
so Lewes's favourite. And mine.
Ah, Burton. We took him to Italy, where he did not disappoint.

I watch him watching me. By the time we come back,
he has it planned: soft chalks, and pastels.
My listening-with-interest-while-forming-a-question pose.

While he, unfortunate man, studies my features, I study his.
His 'Meeting on the Turret Stairs' stirs me to the core.
I must watch myself.

1877, aged 58
Princess Louise, daughter of Queen Victoria

'Old Dame' sketched by a princess
no less, behind my back. The price of fame,
when royalty needs to 'snap' one!
Not flattering – full profile the worst possible angle –
but I was flattered. Am.

From childhood I worked
to make my writing become me.

Rembrandt's mother was probably always beautiful.

Julia Deakin

An angel beguiled

After Middlemarch *(1871-72)*

Picture a man – his intellect pristine,
his brain labyrinthine.

I will ease his lonely labours,
liquefy myself, nourish his roots.

Trinkets rejected, plainly clothed,
I please him with my submission.

When I give myself to this man,
our future hardens.

Affection dwindles and dries. My leaves wilt.
His great work gapes, undone.

Words brighten to invisible.
The pencil's heft buckles my fingers.

Promise me, he says. *Obey my will.*
Make a blank cheque of your soul.

Surrender readied, I enter the garden.
Gravel pours me to the summerhouse.

He is slumped over the stone table,
and there is nothing of him left to serve.

Lucy Dixcart

Well wadded with stupidity

If we had a keen vision and feeling of all ordinary human life, it would be like hearing the grass grow and the squirrel's heart beat, and we should die of that roar which lies on the other side of silence. As it is, the quickest of us walk about well wadded with stupidity. – Middlemarch *(1871-2)*

Every day there is something you take umbrage at.
Your taking-offense antennae are so fine-tuned
that I can hardly ask you to change your shirt,
or please don't boil my breakfast egg too long,
when out spews a bellyful of lies, a shouting gale,
a weather warning of what might lie beneath.
And then, Jack back in the box, the silence,
the sound of a squirrel's heartbeat my only
company, the only breath of a living thing.
I am one who hears the grass grow, I am
aware of the roar on the other side of silence,
and your silence is so profound, so pervasive,
and so long. I wonder what's fermenting,
what mysterious hatred fuels your days,
what I might do or say tomorrow, what will
happen when the barrel bursts, what body
parts and blood will I be buried under,
what vicious dreams, what ill-conceived
revenge brews in the witch's cauldron of
your silent mind. You tell me to say nothing
is better than to say the wrong thing, but
this is intimidation pure and simple.
I hear your tumultuous heartbeat, I know
your sorrow and your pain, they are as
loud to me as your kind smile, your warm
brown eyes, your running around after me
doing make-up jobs. If you could only listen
to the roar, you'd see that wrong things said
can be unsaid, that sharing pain takes shouting
down a notch or two, that love is here to soothe

and heal. You would feel at last the grass start
growing in the watered desert of your heart.

Rosemary McLeish

Mr Eliot

It was *Mr* Eliot as far as I was concerned,
why would I have reason to think otherwise.
Mrs Stockwell had us reading a page each,
voices trailing round the classroom until
my turn, my pleasure to read at long last.

I couldn't understand why some dreaded
the call to read, shuddered inside as voices
got nearer. At least we *could* read, not like
some of them in his books; poor urchins
ground into the land like country fossils.

When I found out George was a woman
I felt betrayed. She had hidden amongst
the rows of desks, cowering like a nervous
reader, afraid of her higher pitch, cheating
us into thinking a man had such imagination.

This was a girls' grammar school. Ambition
shone out of us like a hundred bright moons.
We were destined for doctor's brass plaques,
business cards, trophies, even book shelves.
Your turn George, Georgie, Georgina Elliot.

Pat Edwards

Writing for grown-ups

Middlemarch ... is one of the few English novels written for grown-up people. – Virginia Woolf (TLS, 1919)

What does it take? Certainly passion,
rooted in awareness of blighted hope,
human unfairness; the urge to say,
noticing the science of how things go
– not today's obsessive racket,
but how mind grew, grain by grain
into a sharp, frail reef of knowing;
the skill to choose an image wisely –
a miser stops for a child at the door,
not a dog whistle thief or letter-box
conjured for a chancer's trick;
clearly an ear for human talking,
and what it shows of vanity and longing,
for the music of words and how they dance or lie;
a generous gaze, a beach-comer's eye
or Victorian collector's, searching the sand
to pick a memory, picture, phrase
and find a form to carry home the tale.
How we need you now, and some Grown Ups,
now the vote reform won is undermined
by media boss and corporate lobby,
now our fragile world is locked and loaded.

Terry Simpson

The Long Silence

I have much pleasure in availing myself of the present opportunity to break the long silence which has existed between us. – Letter to Eliot from her brother, Isaac Evans, 17th May 1880.
... our long silence has never broken the affection for you which began when we were little ones. – Eliot's reply, 26th May 1880.

They were too close. The child's
tin can telephone didn't work
if the string was slack. They had to move
further away. They walked backwards
in opposite directions until it was
taut. She cupped the can to her ear to feel,
not hear, the buzz of his voice
pulse down the line. It jarred
through her hammer, anvil and stirrup,
tingled her auricle so she could hardly
bear it. But they were greedy
for each other, her boy and she. The line
pulled too tight and snapped, the sisal
frayed and unravelled. Then the long

silence set in between them,
sat between them with pricked
ears and bared teeth, a shaggy and sour
creature made of frayed string,
an absence so palpable, it growled
itself into presence. After twenty-three years

it lost its bite. For him, a fumbling
with a ring, watched over by a man
in a dusty black frock, rehitched
her broken knot, restored a faint whisper
down a noduled and imperfect cord. But
for her the silence did not end: her shout
bounced back at her from an empty container

pierced by a wick, a Manx stump,
where her line had been severed.

Melanie Branton

Eliot meets Maggie through the looking glass

Ah, our brothers, Maggie. You had Tom.
Childhood friends, dream-worlds apart.
Mine, Isaac, silent as thick ice.
I wash my hands of you for ever, he wrote,
stone-jagged words.

You hacked that thick black hair.
I changed my name.
I, a late bloomer, you, a bullied duckling,
searching for our place,
beyond small-town slurs and snubs.

Our aunts declared, *it's for your own good I say this...*
Yes, we are outcasts looking in.
You are me, Maggie,
questing for a brother's consent.

Maggie Mackay

On the other side of silence

He wrote a scowl of disapproval
and disappeared into silence,
a figment of a brother.

We were two buds that kiss,
a story that began in innocence
and then hit a blank.

All she could imagine for them
was a drowning. Words sank unsaid
in deaf and dumb depths of time.

They were invisible to each other;
whether he wrestled with his stiff faith
for leave to forgive, she did not know.

Her marriage broke the wall.
I wish you happiness and comfort.
With kind love and every good wish.

He waded towards her
through the shallows of propriety,
no death-embrace after all.

Her ink smiled back at him:
Dear Isaac, dear brother.
She wrote of her 'affection',

silence had lasted too long for love.

Derek Sellen

The title comes from *Middlemarch*. Line 4 is based on a line from 'Brother and Sister'.
Lines 14 and 15 are from Isaac Evans' letter of reconciliation (1880).

The true seeing is within

Here in Rome, Cleopatra reclines
in marble voluptuousness, drapery
folding around her with a petal-like ease,
an antique beauty arrested in complete
contentment of her sensuous perfection.
Beside her stands a breathing, blooming girl.

She's clad in Quakerish grey, her cloak thrown
back, one ungloved hand pillowing her cheek,
a white beaver bonnet haloing her face,
her simply braided dark-brown hair,
her large eyes fixed dreamily on
sunlight falling across the gallery floor.

A German painter might dress her as a nun,
exaggerating the visual antithesis,
the idealised sensuality of the statue,
the controlled Christian passion of the living figure,
but he would not express in paint
the true turmoil in this woman's heart.

Only I, with my all-knowing female hand,
can explore for you her inward sight,
the English fields and elms of home,
the hedge-bordered highroads, the joy
of devotion in her new marriage clouding
over, days of dull forlornness closing in.

Clare Wigzell

The title quotation and most of the words and ideas come from chapters XIX, XX
and XXI of *Middlemarch* (1871-72).

Biographies

Veronica Aaronson is the co-founder and one of the organisers of the Teignmouth Poetry Festival. Her work has been published widely in literary journals, online and in anthologies. Veronica's first collection, *Nothing About The Birds Is Ordinary This Morning*, was published by Indigo Dreams in 2018. https://www.indigodreams.co.uk/veronica-aaronson/4594449130

Amina Alyal has published two collections, *The Ordinariness of Parrots* (Stairwell Books 2015) and *Season of Myths* (Indigo Dreams 2016), has published widely including in *The Valley Press Anthology of Yorkshire Poetry*, *Moving Worlds*, *Dream Catcher*, *Iota*, *Envoi*, regularly contributes to Beautiful Dragons anthologies, and has published edited volumes and academic articles, including with NAWE. She is guest editor for *Dream Catcher*. She regularly performs collaboratively with music and poetry, currently with Karl Baxter and Oz Hardwick, previously with the Japanese drumming group Kaminari UK. She lectures in English and Creative Writing at Leeds Trinity University, and is currently writing on ghosts and ecosystems.

Bob Beagrie has published numerous collections of poetry and several pamphlets, most recently *Civil Insolencies* (Smokestack 2019), *Remnants* written with Jane Burn (Knives, Forks & Spoons Press 2019) *Leasungspell* (Smokestack 2016) and *This Game of Strangers* – written with Jane Burn (Wyrd Harvest Press 2017) His work has appeared in numerous anthologies and magazines and has been translated into Finnish, Urdu, Swedish, Dutch, Spanish, Estonian and Karelian. He lives in Middlesbrough and is a senior lecturer in creative writing at Teesside University.

Terri Brandmueller is a poet and writer currently working on a creative non-fiction book about family secrets and Internet genealogy. Her poetry and fiction have appeared in various publications in the US, Canada, and the UK; including *Ambit*, *Barrow Street*, and *The Toronto Quarterly*. She studied literature and cultural studies at the New School for Social Research in NYC, and has an MA in Media Studies. She lives in Vancouver, Canada where she holds a monthly reading salon.

Jo Brandon was born in 1986 and is based in West Yorkshire. Jo has a pamphlet, *Phobia*, and a full-length collection, *The Learned Goose*, with Valley Press. Her third book, *Cures*, is due out in 2021. Jo's poetry has been published widely in magazines including *The North*, *Poetry Review*, *Butcher's Dog*, *Magma*, *Dream Catcher*, *Words for the Wild*, *Dear Damsels*, *The Fenland Reed* and *Popshot*. Jo is a former editor of

Cadaverine and was Bradford Literature Festival's first Digital Poet in Residence. Find out more at: www.jobrandon.com

Melanie Branton is a spoken word artist from North Somerset. She has two collections, *Can You See Where I'm Coming From?* (Burning Eye 2018) and *My Cloth-Eared Heart* (Oversteps 2017), and has been published in journals including *Ink, Sweat & Tears, Bare Fiction, The Frogmore Papers* and *London Grip*. She has previously worked as an assistant theatre director and an English and Drama lecturer and has loved George Eliot's novels since watching a television adaptation of *The Mill on the Floss* when she was ten. *Romola* (the one nobody else likes) is her favourite.

Carole Bromley is a York-based poet, winner of a number of prizes, including the Bridport and the 2019 Hamish Canham Award. She has three collections with Smith/Doorstop, a recent pamphlet, *Sodium 136*, from Calder Valley Poetry and a new collection, *The Peregrine Falcons of York Minster* will be published by Valley Press in September 2020. Carole is an Arvon tutor and mentors for the Poetry School and the Poetry Society.

Anne Caldwell is a poet and lecturer with the Open University. Her latest collection is *Painting the Spiral Staircase* (Cinnamon), and her work has been widely anthologised in the UK and internationally. She is based in West Yorkshire and co-edited *The Valley Press Anthology of Prose Poetry* with Oz Hardwick (2019). She is also completing a PhD in Creative Writing at The University of Bolton. Twitter @caldwell_anne

Anna Chilvers lives in Yorkshire, but comes from Nuneaton. She is a writer, a runner, a long-distance walker, a mother, a teacher and a reader. She has two published novels, *Tainted Love*, (Bluemoose Books, 2016) and *Falling Through Clouds* (Bluemoose Books, 2010). Her third novel will be published in 2020. A few of her poems have appeared in journals. She has written a collection of short stories, *Legging It* (Pennine Prospects, 2012) and her play *The Room* was performed in the Hebden Bridge Arts Festival 2013. She is currently studying for a PhD on novel writing and walking in woodland.

Paul Coleman was born in Somerset sometime during the last Millennium. He might describe himself as a musician, teacher and writer. After staring up the skirts of literary academia for a bit too long, he spent many years teaching English in a High Security Prison. Afterwards, he relocated to rural France with his long-suffering wife and daughter where he now divides his time between teaching, reading, writing, drinking, playing a bit too loudly in bar bands and trying to explain to the locals what the phrase "back of beyond" means.

Mark Connors is an award-winning poet and novelist from Leeds, UK. Mark has had over 170 poems published in magazines, anthologies and webzines. His debut poetry pamphlet, *Life is a Long Song* was published by OWF Press in 2015. His first full length collection, *Nothing is Meant to be Broken*, was published by Stairwell Books in 2017. His second poetry collection, *Optics*, was published in 2019 by Yaffle. His novels, *Stickleback* and *Tom Tit and the Maniacs*, were published in 2016 and 2018. Mark is also a compere, a literary facilitator and a managing editor at Yaffle.

Seth Crook has taught philosophy at various universities, is transitioning into a seal, lives on Mull. His poems have appeared in such places as *The Rialto, Magma, Envoi, The Interpreter's House, Butcher's Dog, Northwords Now, Causeway, Snakeskin*. And in anthologies such as the *Port* (Dunlin Press), *Trio* (Cinnamon), *New Boots and Pantisocracies* (Smokestack Books), *Songs Of Other Places* (ASLS)

Simon Currie, born in Leeds in 1938, in 1970 became a consultant neurologist in Leeds, retired in 1994 then did a PhD on the interaction between European and indigenous medical practitioners in colonies, notably British India and West Indies 1750 to 1900. He wrote poetry, with guidance from a friend in Wales, R. S. Thomas, from 1971 onwards, but went to the Poetry Business (now in Sheffield) in 1999 and had a pamphlet through that in 2010 and a collection in 2013. He is in the Pennine Poets, Otley and Beehive groups. He is to get a further collection (from Yaffle) in 2020. He has done work as a medieval landscape surveyor and botanist in the Yorkshire Dales and elsewhere. He has lived near Otley since 1976. He attends Stanza meetings as well as those other poetry groups, rather sporadically now.

Julia Deakin was born in the George Eliot Hospital, Nuneaton in 1956 and worked her way north to Yorkshire via Shropshire, the Potteries and Manchester. She has won numerous prizes and featured twice on Poetry Please. Each of her collections is praised by leading UK poets. 'Crafted, tender poems, written with passion and purpose,' said Simon Armitage of her first; her fourth, *Sleepless* (Valley Press 2019) is commended by Gillian Clarke. She is the editor of *Pennine Platform* magazine. www.juliadeakin.co.uk

Reverend Professor **Jane de Gay** is Professor of English Literature at Leeds Trinity University and Co-Director (with Professor Karen Sayer) of the Leeds Centre for Victorian Studies. She is the author of *Virginia Woolf and Christian Culture* (Edinburgh University Press 2018), and *Virginia*

Woolf's Novels and the Literary Past (Edinburgh University Press 2006), which examines Woolf's creative responses to a variety of precursors, including George Eliot.

Lucy Dixcart lives in rural Kent. Her poems have appeared in a number of magazines and anthologies, including *Acumen*, *Marble Poetry*, *Eye Flash Poetry*, *The Blue Nib* and *Pale Fire*, an anthology by The Frogmore Press. She was shortlisted for the Canterbury Festival Poet of the Year competition in 2019 and has an MA in Creative Writing from Bath Spa University. @lucydixcart

Pat Edwards is a writer, reviewer, and workshop leader. Her poetry has been published by *Magma*, *Prole*, *Ink Sweat & Tears*, *Atrium* and others. Pat hosts Verbatim poetry open mic nights in venues on the Powys / Shropshire border and she curates Welshpool Poetry Festival. Her debut pamphlet, *Only Blood*, was published by Yaffle Press in 2019, and her next is out later this year with Indigo Dreams.

Barbara Farley was born in Reading but has spent most of her writing life in Budleigh Salterton, Devon. After retiring from teaching, she gained an MA in Creative Writing (with distinction) from Exeter University. She has won both the Sidmouth and Exeter poetry competitions and her poems have appeared in various anthologies. In 2009, she was commissioned to write *Swimmers*, which was broadcast to the nation from Anthony Gormley's Fourth Plinth in Trafalgar Square. She is a regular performer at Exeter's Uncut Poets.

Mike Farren's poems have appeared in journals including The *Interpreter's House*, *Strix* and *Dream Catcher*, and anthologies from Valley Press and Smith/Doorstop. He has been 'canto' winner for Poem of the North, shortlisted for the Bridport Prize and runner-up in The Blue Nib's Chapbook Contest. He is part of the Yaffle publishing team and co-hosts Rhubarb open mic in Shipley. He has published two pamphlets, *Pierrot and his Mother* (Templar, 2017) and *All of the Moons* (Yaffle, 2019). Poems from latter pamphlet were set to music by Keely Hodgson and have been performed at Ilkley Literature Festival and elsewhere.

Adriana Grigore is a writer of fiction who has recently started dabbling in poetry. She has a BA in English Literature and Linguistics and an MA in Literary Translations from the University of Bucharest. In her free time, she attends folklore workshops and tentatively studies herbalism.

Oz Hardwick is a York-based poet, photographer, and occasional musician, whose work has been published and performed internationally in and on diverse media. His chapbook *Learning to Have Lost* (Canberra: IPSI, 2018) won the 2019 Rubery International Book Award for a poetry collection, and has been followed by *The Lithium Codex* (Clevedon: Hedgehog, 2019). He has edited or co-edited several anthologies, most recently *The Valley Press Anthology of Prose Poetry* (Scarborough: Valley Press, 2019) with Anne Caldwell. Oz is Professor of English at Leeds Trinity University, where he leads the Creative Writing MA programme. www.ozhardwick.co.uk

Ian Harker is a co-editor of *Strix* magazine. His pamphlet, *A-Z of Superstitions*, is coming out with Yaffle in 2020.

Angi Holden is a retired lecturer and freelance writer, whose work includes prize-winning adult and children's poetry, short stories and flash fiction, published in online and print anthologies. She brings a wide range of personal experience to her writing, alongside a passion for lifelong learning. She is a former co-editor of the National Flash Fiction Day anthology. Her pamphlet *Spools of Thread*, published in 2018, won the inaugural Mother's Milk Pamphlet Prize. Her work has been published in the Cheshire Prize for Literature poetry and short story anthologies. In 2019 she won the Victoria Baths Splash Fiction competition.

Temidayo Jacob is a Sociologist who writes from the North Central part of Nigeria. He writes as African voice through a global view and his works explore the connection between poetry, humans and society. He is passionate about espousing the conflict between the individual and society, especially through identity, sexuality and conformity. Temidayo Jacob is a Publisher at foenix press. He is the author of *Beauty Of Ashes*. Currently, he is a curator at Artmosterrific. Temidayo's works have appeared and are forthcoming in *Rattle*, *Outcast Magazine*, *Lucent Dreaming*, *Kalahari Review*, *Peeking Cat Poetry*, *Sub-Saharan Magazine*, *Page Adventure*, and others. He is also a contributor to leading anthologies. You can reach him on Twitter @BoyUntouched.

Anna Kisby is a Devon-based poet, archivist and author of the pamphlet *All the Naked Daughters* (Against the Grain Press, 2017). She won the Binsted Arts prize 2019, BBC Proms Poetry competition 2016, and was commended in the Faber New Poet Scheme 2015-16. Her poetry appears in magazines and anthologies, most recently *The Emma Press Anthology of Contemporary Gothic Verse* and *Finished Creatures* journal. In 2019 she was a researcher in Creative History at Bristol University, and is subsequently working on a collection about historical magical practitioners.

Gill Lambert is a poet and teacher from Yorkshire. She has been widely published online and in print and her first collection *Tadaima* was published by Yaffle in 2019.

Sharon Larkin's *Interned at the Food Factory* was published by Indigo Dreams in 2019. Her poems have been anthologised by Cinnamon, Eyewear, Smokestack and more, and regularly appear in magazines such as *Prole* and *Obsessed with Pipework*, and on-line e.g. *Ink Sweat & Tears* and *Atrium*. She has a poem forthcoming in *Magma*. Sharon organizes Poetry Café Refreshed, is Gloucestershire's Stanza Representative and runs Eithon Bridge, publishing anthologies such as *All a Cat Can Be* (2018), *Invisible Zoos* (2019) and *Poetry from Gloucestershire* (2020). Sharon has a Creative Writing MA and is passionate about Wales, photography and the natural world. http://sharonlarkinjones.com

Maggie Mackay loves family and social history which she winds into poems and short stories in print and online journals. She is a MA graduate of The Writing School at Manchester Metropolitan University. One of her poems is included in the award-winning *#MeToo* anthology while others have been nominated for The Forward Prize, Best Single Poem and for the Pushcart Prize. Another was commended in the Mothers' Milk Writing Prize. Her pamphlet *The Heart of the Run* is published by Picaroon Poetry and the booklet *Sweet Chestnut* published by Karen Little in aid of animal welfare. She is a poetry pamphlet reviewer for www.sphinxreview.co.uk

Rosemary McLeish is a 74-year-old artist and poet who started writing about thirty years ago while riding a bike around London. She has had many poems published in magazines, anthologies and podcasts and has won a number of prizes. Her first collection, *I am a field*, was published last year and a new collection, *Defragmentation*, is due out in early 2020. She also writes memoirs and short stories. She first encountered George Eliot over fifty years ago and has been a fan ever since. Further details can be found on her website http://rosemarymcleish.co.uk/.

Rosemary Mitchell is Professor Emerita of Victorian Studies at Leeds Trinity University and a former Director of the Leeds Centre for Victorian Studies. She is the co-author with Hannah Stone of a poetry collection, *Holding Up Half the Sky* (2019), and is currently training for the Anglican ministry with the College of St Hild.

Katrina Naomi's third poetry collection, *Wild Persistence*, will be published by Seren in June 2020. Her poetry has appeared on Poems on the Underground, BBC Radio 4's *Front Row* and in the *TLS*. She was the first writer-in-residence at the Brontë Parsonage Museum in W Yorks. Katrina has been highly commended in the Forward Prize for Poetry and her most recent collection, *The Way the Crocodile Taught Me*, was chosen by Foyles Bookshop as one of its #FoylesFive for poetry. She has a PhD in creative writing from Goldsmiths and teaches for Arvon and the Poetry

School. Katrina is travelling to Mexico shortly to begin work on a new poetry project. www.katrinanaomi.co.uk

Matt Nicholson is a poet and performer from East Yorkshire, from where the culture comes from in these crazy, mixed up times. His two poetry collections to date, *There and back to see how far it is* and *We are not all blessed with a hat-shaped head*, bristle with poems that are sometimes dark and intense, sometimes lyrical and tender, but always painstakingly honest. He has performed all over the country and is a rare, unapologetic voice. Matt's 3rd collection, *Small havocs*, will be published by Yaffle Press in March 2020.

Jenny Robb lives in Liverpool and has been writing poetry since her teens but only seriously since retiring. She is an ex social worker/manager and NHS Director. She has published poems in *The Morning Star*, *The Beach Hut*, and in issue V of *Nightingale & Sparrow* literary magazine.

Anne Ryland's first poetry collection, *Autumnologist*, was shortlisted for The Forward Prize for Best First Collection, and her second, *The Unmothering Class*, was selected for New Writing North's Read Regional Campaign. She recently completed her third collection. Her poems have been published in journals including *Poetry Review*, *Oxford Poetry*, *Magma*, *The North*, *Agenda* and *Long Poem Magazine*, and in anthologies such as *Land of Three Rivers* (Bloodaxe) and *The Valley Press Anthology of Prose Poetry* (Valley Press). She lives in Northumberland and works as a writing facilitator in a range of community settings. https://anneryland.co.uk

Natalie Scott is an internationally published poet from the North East. Her latest collection *Rare Birds – Voices of Holloway Prison* (Valley Press 2020) features 'Colonel Barker', longlisted for the Live Canon Poetry Competition 2018, and 'Katie Gliddon', Highly Commended in the Yaffle Poetry Prize 2019. Her poems were set to music by a team of award-winning British composers and performed by a West End cast at Soho Theatre, supported by the Arts Council of England. As well as managing freelance projects, Natalie loves her role as Lecturer in Creative Writing at Arts University Bournemouth. www.nataliescott.co.uk

Derek Sellen's writing has won awards over the years including first prizes in Poets Meet Politics, Poetry Pulse, Rhyme International, Canterbury Festival Poet of the Year and O'Bheal Five Words. His poems on Jane Austen were recognised in the Wells and CCCU competitions, so he's pleased now to write on George Eliot. His collection *The Other Guernica* (Cultured Llama Publishing, 2018) has been favourably reviewed – '... a work of outstanding richness and variety, imagination, thought, storytelling, full of vivid imagery and the pleasures of language' (Professor Janet Montefiore). Details of his collection are at: http://www.culturedllama.co.uk/books/the-other-guernica

Penny Sharman is a qualified Complimentary Therapist with over twenty years' experience. She is also a counselor, a healer and an awesome cook! Penny is a photographer and artist, but her focus for over fifteen years has been writing poetry. Penny has an MA in Creative Writing from Edge Hill University. She has had over a hundred poems published in magazines such as *The Interpreter's House*, *Obsessed with Pipework*, *Strix*, *The North*, *Ink Sweat & Tears* and Beautiful Dragons Anthologies. Penny's pamphlet *Fair Ground* (Yaffle Press 2019) and her first collection *Swim With Me In Deep Water* (Cerasus Poetry 2019) are available to buy from her website: https://pennysharman.co.uk/. Penny's second collection is to be published in 2020/2021 by Knives Forks & Spoons Press.

Terry Simpson is a musician and writer from Leeds where he has edited several books, including Do*orways in the Night: Stories from the Threshold of Recovery* (Local Voices 2004). Two of his plays have been filmed for use on Open University courses, including a dark musical comedy *An Untimely Death on Passchendaele Ward*. His first solo collection of poetry, *The Magpie's Box*, was published by Yaffle in 2019.

Edwin Stockdale has an MA in Creative Writing (Distinction) from the University of Birmingham. Two of his pamphlets have been published by Red Squirrel Press: *Aventurine* (2014) and *The Glower of the Sun* (2019). He has recently been published by *Atrium*, *Ink Sweat & Tears*, *The Interpreter's House*, *The London Magazine*, *Long Poem Magazine*, *Obsessed with Pipework*, *Orbis*, *Poetry Salzburg Review*, *Prole*, *Poetry Scotland*, *Snakeskin*, *Stand*, *StAnza's Poetry Map of Scotland*, *The Poetry Village*, *The Writers' Café Magazine* and *Three Drops from a Cauldron*. Currently, he is studying for a PhD in Creative Writing at Leeds Trinity University.

Hannah Stone has published four volumes of poetry, including *Lodestone* (2016), *Missing Miles* (2017) and *Swn y Morloi* (2019). She has published several collaborative volumes, most recently *Holding Up Half The Sky* (2019) and is represented in numerous print and online journals and anthologies, including *The Valley Press Anthology of Prose Poetry*. A graduate of the MA in Creative Writing from Leeds Trinity University, Hannah convenes Nowt but Verse and the Leeds Lieder Poets and Composers Forum; she hosts Wordspace open mic. Hannah collaborates with composers Matthew Oglesby and Fiona Pacey.

Kathleen Strafford is an award-winning poet widely published in anthologies and webzines. She has published two poetry collections: *Her Own Language* (Dempsey and Windle 2018), and *Wilderness of Skin* (Yaffle Press 2019). Kathleen is the chief editor of *Runcible Spoon Webzine*, and hosts Runcible Spoon open mic in Morley, Leeds, the second Sunday of each month.

Jean Taylor lives in Edinburgh. Her poetry has been published in a range of publications including *Pushing Out the Boat*, *Southlight*, *Orbis*, *Northwords Now*, *Firth* and *Envoi* as well as in anthologies and online in *Atrium*, *Snakeskin*, *Amaryllis*, *The Writer's Café* and *Ink Sweat & Tears*. Her pamphlet *Deliberate Sunlight* was published by Black Agnes Press in 2019.

Sally Taylor is from Hampshire. She attended Derby Art School 1993-1995. She holds MA in Creative Writing, (Distinction), University of Nottingham. She also holds BA (Hons) Literature, (First), The Open University. Her poem 'Full Blown' won 'The Word', Lichfield Cathedral Poetry Competition (26 years+) November 2019. She writes short stories, plays and life-writing. Sally is creator and facilitator of RICHES (Rhymes In Care Homes and Educational Settings). She is currently seeking representation for a MG novel, *The Deep Blue Sea*. She regularly submits to poetry competitions and zines and is always looking forward to her next project.

Angela Topping is the author of eight full collections of poetry and four pamphlets. She is a former Writer in Residence at Gladstone's Library. Her poems have featured on Poetry Please, been set for A level and included in over 100 anthologies. She has been published in many journals including *Poetry Review*, *Magma*, *The North* and *Stand*.

Stephen Wade has been writing poetry for many years. His first collection, *Churwell Poems*, was published by Littlewood in 1987. His next is *Stretch*, from Smokestack, a collection about his work as a writer in prisons. His involvement in poetry has included many years writing for *Agenda*, *Acumen* and other journals.

Paul Waring lives on the Wirral. His poems have been published in a range of print journals, anthologies and webzines. In 2019, he was awarded second place in the inaugural Yaffle Prize, commended and shortlisted in the Welshpool Poetry Competition and had a debut pamphlet *Quotidian*, published by Yaffle Press.

Clint Wastling's poetry has been published in *Blue Nib*, *Dream Catcher*, *Strix*, *Marble* and online with *The Algebra of Owls*. Most recently a pamphlet entitled *Layers*, has been published by Maytree Press. His novel, *The Geology of Desire*, is an LGBTQ thriller set around Whitby in the 1980's and Hull during World War II. He also has a sci-fi novel, *Tyrants Rex*. Both are available from Stairwell Books.

Sarah Watkinson's debut pamphlet, *Dung Beetles Navigate by Starlight* (Cinnamon, 2017) was a winner in the Cinnamon Press Poetry Pamphlet Competition. A plant scientist, she is currently writer in residence at Wytham Woods, and leads Oxford University's TORCH SciPo New Network for science poetry. She lives in West Oxfordshire, close to the old quarry for Bladon Forest Marble.

Gail Webb's passion for poetry reignited later in life. Life as a social worker and a mother of two children has been absorbing. Gail relishes opportunities through poetry to share experiences she thought were long dissipated, to make sense of a hurting world and find some joy in the small things. Published last year in feminist journal *Boshemia* and in the anthology *Write Like A Girl* (2019). As a child Gail read an abridged version of *The Mill on The Floss*, inherited from her mother, and still has the book! Hence her poem in celebration of George Eliot.

Clare Wigzell, a Leeds-based poet, performs regularly at open mic events, such as Wordspace and Runcible Spoon. She was successful in her MA in Creative Writing at Leeds Trinity University and has been published in anthologies with Indigo Dreams. She performed and published a long poem with Leeds City Council, *Walking Kirkstall Abbey*. She has completed a chapbook about Barbara Hepworth, which she is performing in art galleries. She collaborates with book artist Lynette Willoughby under the name Rock Tree Landscape. She collaborates with two other poets, Hannah Stone and Emma Barr, exploring spirituality in poetry.

Joe Williams is a writer and performing poet from Leeds. In 2017 his debut pamphlet, *Killing the Piano*, was published by Half Moon Books, and he won the Open Mic Competition at Ilkley Literature Festival. His second book, the verse novella *An Otley Run* (2018) was shortlisted in the Best Novella category at the 2019 Saboteur Awards. His poems and short stories have been included in numerous anthologies, and in magazines online and in print. Despite all of that, he is probably most widely read thanks to his contributions to *Viz*. www.joewilliams.co.uk www.anotleyrun.com